kabatalemwa

Belongs to Those Who Cannot be Defeated

Gertrude Kabatalemwa

with
Teresa Skinner

illustrated by
Jackson Muthoni

Kabatalemwa

Belongs to Those Who Cannot be Defeated

contents

my story

Growing up

This is a true story about Kasoya Adyeri a little girl who was born in Tooro Kingdom, in Western Uganda.

Uganda had cultural kings, so when the British came to colonize Uganda, they found there was good administration through kingdoms. Instead of making Uganda a Colony, the British made it a Protectorate because of these administrative skills.

My grandfather was an uncle to the King. When my father, Simeon Rwakihoza Kachope, was 23 years old and knew how to read and write, his father took him to the King, and the King made him a Crown Chief. The royals and close clans to the royals were made administrators.

Later my father was posted as a Parish Chief by King George Rukidi, the King of Tooro to Kilembe and later to Bwera counties bordering Congo.

I was born on 16th May 1946 to Mr Kachope and Auralia K. Kachope at a place called Kilembe, which turned into Copper Mines in 1954. I was the second born in the family.

As a custom, when a child was born, the young couple was not allowed to name the child when the new father's father was still alive, so after a month, my parents traveled back to the Nyamabuga village, a two-hour drive, but at that time, it used to take them three to four hours due to bad roads and scarce transport. My grandfather was the head of the big clan next to the ruling clan and a maternal uncle to King George Rukidi. He commanded great respect among the subjects of the Kingdom.

Normally when a child was born, they would wait for 3 days for a girl and 4 days for a boy to give her or him a name. In my case, it took a month as my father and mum were far from the village. I was named by my grandfather, and a party was thrown for members of the family and neighbours as, at that time, there was enough food, meat, and local brew to celebrate. I was named **Kabatalemwa;** this means "**the one who belongs to those who cannot be defeated.**"

I was named Kabatalemwa because my grandfather's clan was known as Abatalemwa, meaning "those who cannot be defeated." In those days, tribes and clans used to engage in tribal battles that resulted in great victories, and the loot used to be cows. In fact, anyone considered to be wealthy had to have many heads of cattle. These Bagweri clansmen were called Abatalemwa because they were strong and courageous in all their battles.

I was also given the pet name **Adyeri** by my grandfather. I was so tiny, and my given name was too long. My father nicknamed me "Kasoya Bean" after soya bean, a name which I was called on a daily basis. It came about that at that time, the King of Tooro brought in soya beans and encouraged his subjects to grow them as cash crops.

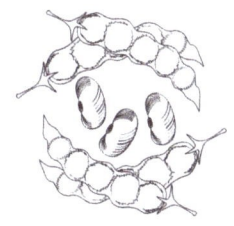

Gertrude Kabatalemwa and cousin

kasoya adyeri

In the Tooro kingdom, there are three special occasions families celebrate before a child reaches 10 years of age: the naming, the teething, and the shaving of hair. Most children born in the families of chiefs did not have their hair shaved until they were ten years old. They used to keep their hair in braids to serve as a treasure collection and a start up capital.

As a little girl, I had a lot of hair, which was styled in braids. My mum, aunts, and grandmother placed a large collection of money, beads, cowrie seashells, buttons, and many other valuables in my hair. It was like a start  up capital for my future. This was our custom, and as I walked with my mum or grandmother, people would stop, admire my hair and decorate it with money. It was considered to be mean to stop a child with braids (Njwenge) and not put something in her hair.

Everyone loved me because of my beautiful hair. At that time in East Africa, all three countries of, Kenya, Uganda,

and Tanzania, used one currency, and
the coins had a hole in the middle,
which made it easy to push the hair
through the coin.

My hair was supposed to be kept for 10
years, but when I started school at the
age of 8, my hair was an attraction to older children at school.
They wanted to take some money to buy pancakes. I had
easy money to pick - with ten cents, one would buy ten
pancakes. This made it difficult for me to continue keeping
my beautiful hair. For one week after starting school, I
returned home crying, so my father decided to shave my hair.

The day they shaved my braids was such a big occasion for
my family, relatives, friends, and neighbours. People were
invited to witness my hair being shaved. Invited relatives and
friends who lived far away came a day before for the
occasion.

On the eve, I was treated as a bride. I was not allowed to do
anything. Girls came to prepare food for the occasion. The
whole house was cleaned and decorated in the morning. The
living room was carpeted with treated soft calves skin called
(enkeeto). In the middle of the room, there were three
beautiful baskets: one to collect money and other valuables
from the hair, which would be later given a value, another
basket with fresh palm leaves to tie the coins, making it easy
to count, and a basket containing a knife for shaving the hair.

Early in the morning, a big meal was prepared, and I was
dressed in my best. At around midday, when all visitors had
arrived, the whole family assembled, and I was brought out
and sat in the middle of the room on a calf's skin, and my

father and grandfather took their seats. My father addressed the people explaining the circumstances that prompted him to shave my hair before the traditional age of 10.

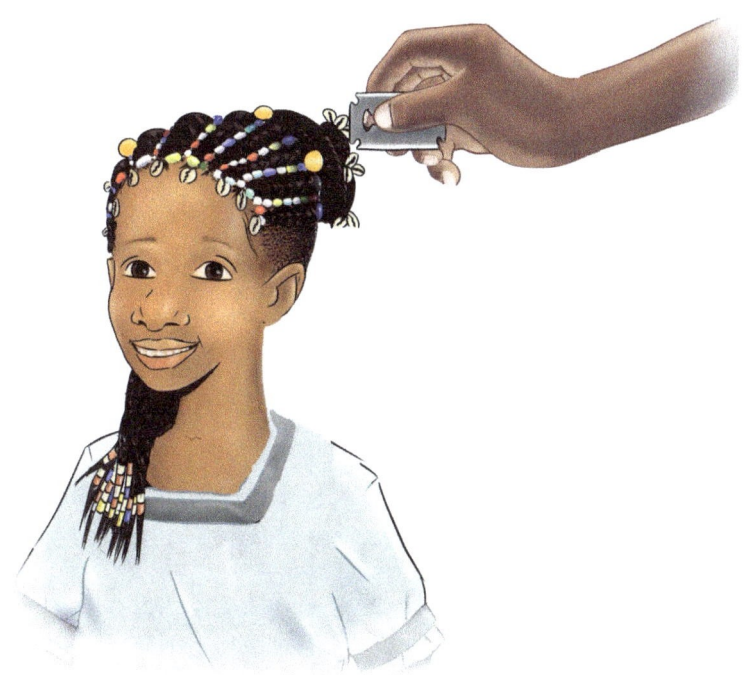

My aunt assisted him and poured water to wet my hair. Then father picked a bundle of hair from the temple of my head and shaved them, and placed them in a basket. Everyone gathered cheered. After that, all my hair was shaved, and people came to give gifts or pledges like cows, goats, or money. These gifts are called "Gifts for Hair." After the gifts, a big dinner was served, accompanied by a big party of drinking and dancing.

The gifts, money, and all valuables which were collected from my hair were given a value, and that was considered a start-up capital. This capital always depends on the wealth of the family. Some families would purchase cows or goats or chickens from the hair.

Kasoya dolls handmade by Gertrude Kabatalemwa

my father

The village of Kihoza (meaning Tax collectors) where I grew up was named as such because the people who were living in this village were tax collectors for my great-grandfather. In fact, the name of my father, Rwahihoza, means that he was born in the village of tax collectors. All herdsmen from Tooro and Bunyoro used to bring their cows to drink from the springs, which was known to have healing properties. If a cow did not give much milk, it was brought to drink from these springs in order to give more milk. But for their cows to be treated, they had to pay some coins for each cow; the total cost would therefore depend on how many cows one herdsman had.

Later in 1949, my father asked to be posted back to his home area. The King accepted and brought him back. As I was growing up, my father, being a chief and good-hearted man, used to bring many orphaned children of relatives and other homeless people to our home. So, my home was always filled with many people and full of activities. We had a big house with a ceiling made of fine reeds, larger than any house around, and it had a fine reeds fence. There was a Court where lawbreakers were brought to be judged, and at times, we would attend the court procession.

Later my brother and my sister were born. Being the children of the chief, we were given special treatment. Men used to work in our compound; women used to bring food for storage, preparing for future times when we'd need food.

There used to be special occasions that would make all of us and many villagers very excited. The King would send his Royal musicians to visit his uncle's homes to entertain them. They would entertain us for a month or two, and this meant eating, drinking, and dancing. Many villagers would assemble every evening to dance and listen to royal music. During this time period, all the subjects of the King were summoned to bring food and brew for these troupes of 10 to 20s. Women would come to do the cooking and serving.

my brother's haircut

When I was young, I was fascinated by razor blades. My father had a special kit to keep his shaving machines and blades. But every moment when we were left alone, I would go to look for razor blades to do surgery on bees and grasshoppers, cutting their abdomen to see what was in there.

I was a bit older than my brother and sister, so I often pretended to be their mum, shaving their foreheads. My father would always find all his razor blades broken, and I would get a good beating from him. Then he started hiding them in the ceiling, but I would still get a mortar, climb on it and reach the door to the ceiling.

It happened one day when father had gone to work. I got the mortar and climbed on it, and reached the door to the ceiling. Carefully stretching, I reached for the razor blade. Now, where was my brother?

I found him and told him, "Sit here. I will shave your head. You look terrible now." My brother squirmed, not confident about my abilities. As he sat quietly, I focused on shaving his hair. "That is better now," I said. But your eyebrows are bushy. We must make them very sharp. My brother flinched as I neared his eyebrow, and then, the eyebrow was completely gone! Oh no, what would Father say? Quickly I shaved the other eyebrow to match while saying nothing to my brother. "Now, you look very sharp. Go and play."

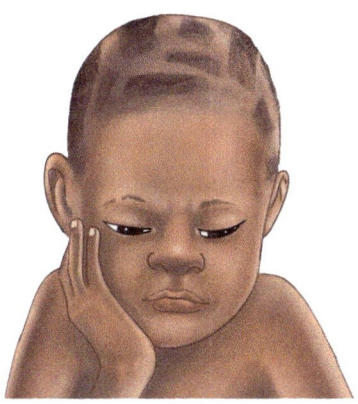

My brother cried and cried. We were both afraid of what Father would say. I quickly placed the razor blade back.

Father came home that night, and we sat down to eat. But where was my brother? It seemed to take a long time for him to finally come to the table. He slipped into his seat at the table. Father took one look at him and said, "Who let that dog in the house while we are eating? Go from the table and do not come back until your hair is grown back."

This time father did not beat me, but the terrible way my brother looked and being isolated at mealtime made me think twice before I shaved anyone's eyebrows again.

teething party

A few months after the birth of a baby, relatives, friends, and neighbours would wait expectantly for the teething party.

As soon as two teeth appear on the lower palate, the family starts to prepare for the party. All relatives, friends, and neighbours are invited to the occasion. That evening, the house is given more attention. The sitting room is carpeted with calves' soft skin after being fumigated and perfumed with sandalwood logs and other smelling incense; a basket with palm leaves is placed on the table for the collection of gifts and teething money. In the morning, a goat or cow is slaughtered, and a meal is prepared. When all the guests assemble, the baby is brought in by his/her mum, and people give gifts like cows, goats, or money. This is called gifting for the teeth. After the meal is served, the money and gifts collected are used to buy livestock for the child.

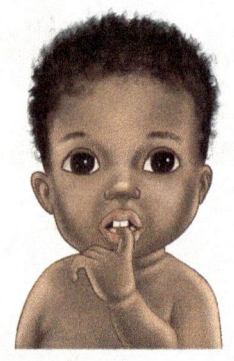

nyamabuga - place of healing springs

My great-grandfathers were close relatives of the King. When the ruling dynasty was immigrating from North Africa, they first settled in Northern Uganda, near Lake Kyoga. This royal clan man had twin boys who were born to him by a woman of the Northern tribe in Uganda called Langis. These boys were born under a Biito tree and were called Kabiito and Kagweri. As they grew up, they wanted to be independent.

One day, Kabiito escaped from his young brother and ran towards Lake Kyoga, where the elders had hidden the canoe. Kabiito started rowing across the lake where the elders were waiting.

His young brother, by instinct, knew that there was a kingdom waiting for them to take on, so he also followed him running but could not catch up with him. He decided to swim across the lake. As soon as Kabiito arrived, the elders sounded the royal drum, and his young brother arrived gasping.

The elders who were gathered appraised him and said huuuuuuu, Kagweri you will be known as "Grabber"!!!!!!!! Because in Kagwer's determination to become royalty he "grabbed" the lake. From this day onwards, Kabiito became Babiito Clan, and Kagweri became the Bagweri Clan. The elders decided that Kagweri should get some share of the royal drums, spears, shields, etc.

After these, the royals settled in Bunyoro Kitara, and they came up with names like Okwiri, Winyi, Wako, Ogen, Ochaki, and Opuuli known in Babiito and Bagweri clans (Royals) and pet names like Akiiki, Amooti, Adyeri, Abooki and many more, which are used commonly in Banyoro and Batooro tribes.

When Batooro broke again from Banyoro to form the Tooro Kingdom in 1830, Babiito, the ruling clan, gave shares to the Bagweri clan. This made my great-grandfather a direct relative to the King; there were intermarriages among them as they wanted to keep their seed; therefore, they gave my great grandfather lands in the area now known as Kyenjojo District Butara and called it Butara bw"Opuuli. In that part of the land, there are Embuga (Hot Springs).

These springs have the ability to heal various diseases in cows and make them produce more milk. Since that area had many hot springs, it was given the name, NYAMABUGA, meaning the **PLACE OF HEALING SPRINGS,** where we have projects and Nyamabuga Foundation Schools.

grandpa kills a lion

My grandpas, both of my maternal and paternal, were cattle keepers. This true story is about my maternal grandfather, who used to graze his cows far away in the hills. At that time, animals like elephants would roam everywhere, destroying people's gardens, and lions would kill cattle and eat people.

One day, when my grandpa was grazing his cows far away in the hills, a lion crawled on its belly to take one of his cows. Grandpa saw the lion in the short grass and prepared to fight the lion so that it would not take his cow.

People who grazed cows used to have a staff and a spear. The lion does not fear the spear, but it fears the staff.

The lion was ready to leap and take the cow, but my grandpa was very smart. He counted the steps between the cow and the lion so that when the lion leaped to grab the cow, grandpa also leaped and stuck his staff in the open mouth of the lion. He fought the lion with his staff until he killed it.

In this story, we learn to be wise and bold and not let people get away with what belongs to us.

kalulu the hare

African folklore

In Africa there lived a very clever cunning small animal called Kalulu. A Kalulu is like the hare, who resembles a rabbit, **but this fellow is wild.**

Once upon a time lived Kalulu the Hare. One day Kalulu decided to go shopping at the market with his friend the elephant.

Happily enough, he found a big bull, but his friend did not, and he bought a small one.

On the way home, Kalulu being so small and walking with a big bull, feared that if he met strong animals on the way, they would grab the bull from him.

So, as they were walking, when they met strong animals like the lion, leopard, or hyena, who asked him, "eh!! Kalulu you have such a big bull?!", he would answer them, "No this bull is not mine. I am helping my friend Elephant. Mine is the small one that the elephant is walking with."

Kalulu and his elephant friend met many strong animals, and he made the same statement until they reached home.

Kalulu knew that sooner or later those strong animals would come to grab his bull. So, he sat down to plan how he was going to trick them.

One morning, Kalulu invited all the strong and dangerous animals that he knew would bring trouble for him, to a party.

Kalulu went into his house and spoke through a loudspeaker with such a big, loud voice to scare the strong and dangerous animals. Kalulu said, "Thus says the king. Today he is going to have a party, he will slaughter his big bull, but first each animal will be given an errand to fulfill.

1. Leopard, you will go and fetch water to boil the meat. A reed basket will be given to you to fetch water. And you must bring the basket back full of water, without one drop escaping.

2. Lion, you are going to split the rocks, which will be used as firewood. You will be given an axe to split the rocks, and the axe should be brought back without any dents!!!

3. Hyena, you are going to slaughter the bull. But you cannot leak even one drop of blood.

Now, everyone pick up your tools, and off to your errands."

When Lion tried to split the rocks with the axe, by the second stroke the axe was already dented. Lion frantically looked for stones to straighten the dents; it took him almost to midday. Lion got so scared that he just left the axe on the rock and ran away. He did not know what to tell the king.

Leopard went to the well. Not even one drop of water could be held by the reed basket! Leopard sat at the well crying, wondering what he was going to tell the king.

Lion passed by to hear his story. When the leopard told him what he had gone through, the lion advised, "let's run before the king finds out." And off they went.

Hyena was busy cutting the meat. When the bone flew into the bush, he would run, pick it, bring it back and put it on a heap. But as he was cutting, one fatty bone flew, and Hyena said, "This one, I will not spare." He pretended he was going to collect it, but instead he picked it up and threw it in his mouth.

Kalulu was watching Hyena and made an alarm that the hyena has disobeyed the king's order. Hyena took off and left the meat right there.

Kalulu the Hare gathered all the meat of his bull. He took it into the house where no animal had any share.

So, Kalulu in his craftiness, had created an imaginary king in order to scare the strong dangerous animals from eating his bull, and Kalulu ended up eating it alone.

about the author

This true story is about "Kasoya Adyeri" - Gertrude Kabatalemwa, a little girl who was born in the Tooro Kingdom, in Western Uganda in 1946. Ms Kabatalemwa enjoyed her childhood. In her own words she shares stories and an African folklore tale.

In the past, Ms. Gertrude Kabatalemwa served her nation as secretary to the president. She also functioned as Minister for the Development of Women.

At one point, she had taken thirty-five orphans into her own village home, subsequently establishing Nyamabuga Foundational Schools for village children. Her vision for the school was to equip young people with the skills necessary to lead their nation with integrity and a godly moral worldview.

Although Ms. Gertrude Kabatalemwa went to be with the Lover of her soul in 2015 her children and trained staff continue her God given vision in Uganda.

This is Gertrude's seventh book.

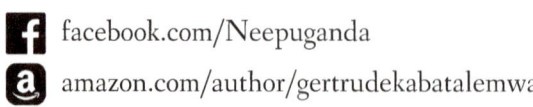

facebook.com/Neepuganda

amazon.com/author/gertrudekabatalemwa